SCOTT JOPLIN

The Easy Winners
A Ragtime Two Step

Maurice Hinson, Editor

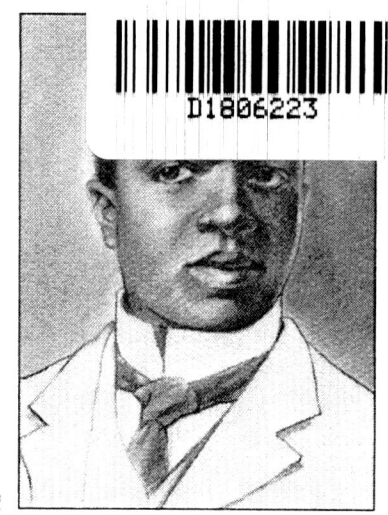

Illustration: Ted Engelbart

About the Composer

Scott Joplin was born in Texarkana, Texas, on November 24, 1868, and died in New York City on April 1, 1917. He was the leading figure in ragtime and a man very much in tune with the times. He is widely considered to be the best of all ragtime composers—the most professional, original and serious composer of this genre. His music is finally receiving its proper acclaim in American literature. The works of Joplin include 53 pieces for piano, 10 songs, and the opera *Treemonisha*.

About the Music and This Edition

Form: Introduction = measures 1–4; **A** = 5–21; **B** = 22–38; **A** = 39–54; bridge = 55–58; **C** = 59–76; **D** = 77–94.

This jaunty piece is one of the favorites from his early period. It sounds fresh with its use of syncopation against a regularly accented bass to provide complex polyrhythms. Not all notes are syncopated in this popular rag but the syncopated notes predominate, so that each musical phrase seems to be set in opposition to the beat.

The introduction (measures 1–4) contains syncopation in measures 1–2; measures 3–4 are "straight" rhythmically, and provide contrast for more syncopation in measures 5–7. Measure 8 is straight, measures 9–19 use syncopation and measures 20–21 are straight. This kind of contrast (syncopation versus no syncopation) is used throughout this rag.

Practice and performance suggestions:

1. This captivatingly melodious rag should move at a very comfortable tempo and avoid sounding rushed.

2. One of the most difficult aspects of rag composition is keeping the left hand steady while being accurate with the large skips. Stay close to the keys to aid with accuracy.

3. The left-hand octaves in measures 12, 58, 59, 62 and similar places should be slightly accented.

4. Separate eighth notes (nonlegato) and connect 16ths for effective ragtime performance style.

Used in the 1973 movie *The Sting*, this rag helped spark a revival of ragtime.

All fingerings are editorial except those indicated in italics in measures 34–35, which are Joplin's. All dynamics and the metronomic indication in parentheses are editorial.

Source: First edition, Scott Joplin, St. Louis, MO, 1901. Also available in Alfred edition nos. 4615 and 445.

This edition is dedicated to Dr. Rick Andrews, with appreciation and admiration.

Maurice Hinson

Second Edition
Copyright © MMIV by Alfred Music.
All rights reserved. Produced in USA.

Cover art: Detail of Manhattan Rhythms, *c. 1915
by Leon Kroll (1881–1974)
Oil on Canvas, 48 ¼" x 36 ¼"
Private collection courtesy of
Gerald Peters Gallery, New York*

The Easy Winners

A Ragtime Two Step

(1901)

Scott Joplin
(1868–1917)

ALFRED MASTERWORK LIBRARY
Most Requested

Bach/18 Short Preludes
(Palmer)
Book (601)
CD (rec. K. O'Reilly) (16790)

Bach/Dances of J. S. Bach (Hinson) (600)

Bach/French Suites (Schneider) (700)

Bach/Two-Part Inventions (Palmer) (604)

**Bach/Inventions and Sinfonias
(Two- and Three-Part Inventions)** (Palmer)
Leather (4867)
Paper (Comb-bound) (606C)
CD (rec. Lloyd-Watts) (4056)

Bach/Selections from Anna Magdalena's Notebook
(Palmer)
Book (605)
CD (rec. Lloyd-Watts) (16792)

Bach/Well-Tempered Clavier, Volume 1
(Palmer) (2098C)

Beethoven/16 of His Easiest Piano Selections (383)

**Beethoven/13 of His Most Popular
Piano Selections** (390)

**Beethoven/Selected Intermediate to Early Advanced
Piano Sonata Movements** (Hinson)
Volume 1 (4841)
Volume 2 (4842)

Burgmüller/18 Characteristic Studies, Op. 109
(Hinson) (4829)

Burgmüller/25 Progressive Pieces, Op. 100 (Palmer)
Book (608)
CD (rec. Lloyd-Watts) (16787)

Chopin/14 of His Easiest Piano Selections (397)

**Chopin/19 of His Most Popular
Piano Selections** (389)

Chopin/Etudes, Complete (Palmer) (2500C)

Chopin/An Introduction to His Piano Works (Palmer)
Book (635)
CD (rec. Lloyd-Watts) (4013)

Chopin/Mazurkas (Palmer) (2481)

Chopin/Nocturnes (Palmer) (2482C)

Chopin/Polonaises, Complete (Palmer) (2480C)

Chopin/Preludes (Palmer) (610)

Chopin/Selected Favorites (Palmer) (611)

Chopin/Waltzes (Palmer) (2483)

Clementi/Six Sonatinas, Op. 36 (Palmer)
Book (609)
CD (rec. K. O'Reilly) (16771)

Czerny/30 New Studies in Technique, Op. 849
(Palmer) (591)

**Czerny/Practical Method for Beginners on
the Piano, Op. 599, Complete** (Palmer) (596)

**Czerny/The Art of Finger Dexterity,
Op. 740, Complete** (Palmer) (595C)

Czerny/The School of Velocity, Op. 299 (Palmer)
Book 1 (613)
Complete (612)

Czerny/The Young Pianist, Op. 823, Complete
(Palmer) (590)

Czerny/Selected Piano Studies, Volume 1
(Germer/Palmer) (597)

Debussy/Children's Corner Suite (Hinson) (667)

Debussy/Preludes, Book 1 (Hinson) (2594)

Debussy/Preludes, Book 2 (Hinson) (2598)

Debussy/Selected Favorites (Olson) (2495)

Hanon/The Virtuoso Pianist (Small)
Book 1 (617)
Book 2 (682)
Complete Edition (616C)
GM Disk, Book 1 (arr. Wren) (5715)

Hanon/Junior Hanon (Small) (518)

Köhler/Sonatina Album (Small)
Book (1710C)
Two CDs (rec. K. O'Reilly) (3997)

**Kuhlau/Nine Sonatinas, Opp. 20 and 55
for the Piano** (Palmer) (4889)

Mendelssohn/Songs without Words, Complete
(Hinson) (4860C)

Mozart/14 of His Easiest Pieces (384)

Mozart/21 of His Most Popular Pieces
(Palmer) (391)

**Mozart/Selected Intermediate to Early Advanced
Piano Sonata Movements** (Hinson) (4884)

Mozart/Six "Viennese" Sonatinas (Palmer) (1707)

Rachmaninoff/10 Preludes, Op. 23 (Baylor) (515)

Rachmaninoff/13 Preludes, Op. 32 (Baylor) (655)

Rachmaninoff/Selected Works (Baylor) (2423)

Satie/Gymnopédies and Gnossiennes (Baylor) (2501)

Schmitt/Preparatory Exercises, Op. 16 (Palmer) (1709)

Schubert/Impromptus, Op. 90 (Baylor) (544)

Schumann/Album for the Young, Op. 68 (Palmer)
Book (620)
Two CDs (rec. K. O'Reilly) (16796)

Schumann/Scenes from Childhood, Op. 15 (Palmer)
Book (632)
CD (rec. Lloyd-Watts) (16794)

Streabbog/12 Melodious Pieces, Book 1, Op. 63
(Palmer) (621)

Tchaikovsky/The Nutcracker Suite, Op. 71a (Hinson)
Duet, 1 Piano/4 Hands (4858)
Solo Piano (4856)
CD (rec. Reed/Reed) (16774)

Tchaikovsky/The Seasons, Op. 37b (Hinson) (4826)

Tchaikovsky/Album for the Young, Op. 39 (Novik) (485)

Tcherepnin/Bagatelles, Op. 5 (Olson) (551)

ISBN-10: 0-7390-2437-X
ISBN-13: 978-0-7390-2437-9

alfred.com

8064 $4.99 in USA

ISBN 0-7390-2437-X